"It is she who paints with flowers that captivates the beams of light, directs the flights of bees and sends blooms skywards, competing with the sun itself all in her garden sanctuary. Always spinning, always bending the matter of the universe with her brush of time. Around and around and around in orbit, dancing like dust in light, like energy around the core, like souls meant to be. It is in this orbit I wish always to remain."

— STEVEN P. BLOOM, in memoriam

"Every once in a while we bump into a writer who invites us into her inner sanctum for a friendly chat. As Sharon Bloom shares her story you find yourself nodding your head in agreement. *Yes*, you say. *Me too.* That's called poetry with a universal appeal. Ready for a friendly chat? Have a seat."

— GORDY WHITEMAN, Guilford Poet Laureate Emeritus

"In Sharon Austin Bloom's nuanced and moving triptych of loss, *Holding the Light*, she takes us on a Dante-like spiritual journey. Rather than hell and heaven, she emphasizes we exist in a world of finding, holding, and losing that which we love—in her case, that most hellish of losses, the death of a child. Instead of being depressing, however, her poems are anything but. The best of them, like those of Blake and Wordsworth, hold out a hope beyond death through the unifying power of love and the holiness of nature."

— MICHAEL C. WHITE, author of *Resting Places*

"With the heart of a mother and the soul of a naturalist, Sharon Bloom brings her readers into the darkest sufferings of loss and offers a way through towards hope and healing. Whether paddling her kayak on a quiet inlet or pulling prickers in her beloved garden, she is a keen observer of nature's ability to glimpse the divine within the ordinary moments of our lives. Her sensitive insight connects us to a deeper truth of what it means to mother — a child, a garden, or ourselves — through all the seasons of our human condition. Bloom's poetic voice reaches for a place where love, loss, shadow, and light find a home together among the marsh marigolds, a mother's memory of a sun-kissed boy, and in the ineffable mysteries of the spiritual realm. That place is one in which the reader is drawn to linger, to wonder, and to be transformed."

— MARIE HULME, English Professor, Sacred Heart University

"Sharon Bloom's poetic perspective manages to be minute yet cosmic. She is imbued with the ways of the Earth but aware of the vastness that surrounds us—both time and space. This book is distinguished by the poet's talent for appreciating the fragility of our lives and the generational persistence of objects, as in the wonderful poem spoken by a wooden spoon. The poet has experienced searing loss but that makes the appreciation all the stronger. This is a very real collection of poems by someone who has come to accept the mystery of our being here, an acceptance tinged with reverence and wonder."

— BARON WORMSER, author of *The History Hotel*

HOLDING THE LIGHT

Holding the Light

Poems by
SHARON AUSTIN BLOOM

Guilford, Connecticut • 2025

Sharon Austin Bloom
sharonbloom925@gmail.com
www.sharonaustinbloom.com

Text and images ©2025, Sharon Austin Bloom unless otherwise noted below.

All rights reserved, unless otherwise noted below. No part of this book may be reproduced or translated in any form or by any means, digital, electronic, or mechanical, including photocopying, recording, or by any information storage and retrieval system, without permission in writing from the publisher, except for the use of brief quotations in a book review or related article.

Author photo by Jarek Strzemien

"Monarch's Return," kieferpix, iStock
"Trees Begin to Weep," Studio Light and Shade, iStock
"Indigo Wings," Steve Byland, iStock
"Skiing in Yellowstone," DW, Adobe Stock

Book Design by Words by Jen (Branford, CT)

Printed in the U.S.A.

ISBN: 979-8-218-81238-6

POE000000   POETRY
POE023030   POETRY / Animals & Nature
POE023010   POETRY / Death, Grief, Loss

For My Sons Matt & Andy

Like many before me, I began writing poetry as a confused teenager. Poetry and journal writing became my refuge. Today I would cringe to read those overwrought poems. Decades later those poems took root, sprouting new shoots fed by the rain of tears and the sunlight of joy. I am honored to share these tender shoots, to hold them to the light and see them grow.

Poetry gave voice to my inner spirit and permission to bear witness to the world around me. Through poetry I am still the child who climbs trees, the young mother struggling the best she can, the passionate woman not afraid to love, the wise crone reflecting on a life fully lived. To remain in the flow of the river of life, I rely on poetry to clear the logjams of grief and woe, as well as to celebrate moments of bliss and days of wonder.

My deepest desire is for this collection to create a bridge between you, me and what is universal. By connecting with the self, with nature and with each other, I invite you to ponder the big questions in life. In a world that spins faster every day, poetry forces us to slow down, to savor every word rather than speed read the latest headlines. Poetry allows us to tap into senses dulled by the buzz of technology and the rapid fire pace of life. It allows us to see ourselves in others, to feel our shared humanity and explore the depths of emotion.

Sharon Austin Bloom

Finding

Watch Hill on Indian Lake

Pine needles soften my step
the uphill climb goes slower now
I still long to scamper up the hillcrest
run pell-mell towards the next
but a watchful gait guides me now

My breath catches as I peer more closely
life teems all around
ghost plants sprout from musty leaves
their pearly fronds unfurl
floating rootless on eons of decay

A fallen tree blocks my path
branches no longer reach for the sky
but they reach all the same
its hollow trunk a weasel's safe haven
its soft pulp a woodpecker's delight

At the summit I bask on sun baked boulders
seeking dragons in the clouds
below an eagle soars on rippling currents
Indian Lake shimmers beyond
adorned by a necklace of mountains

Descending through hemlocks
metallic notes ignite the air
syncopated rain brushes pine boughs,
drums mossy rocks
skims fanning ferns

Orchestral sounds meld in unison
thunderclaps, their adoring audience
lightning, their only conductor
and I, their silent witness

Moon Swallows

An amber crescent peeks over treetops
nudging its way into a dusky sky
the curtain rises, the show begins

The full moon whispers to the sun
should be a good one tonight
the sun dons a cloak of watermelon sky
flashes a tangerine smile and disappears

Moonglow beckons swallows to roost
rustling reeds nod feathery heads
come, find safe haven here

One swallow swoops overhead
dozens skim the surface
racing to this nightly ritual

Thousands swarm smudging the sky
daredevils flit across the moon
they dive and dip in an aerial ballet

A dance of veils pulsing and surging
then vanishing in a whoosh as
the night curtain falls

Like arrows shot from the moon's quiver
they rest amidst the swaying reeds
one night of magic, of mystery, of awe

One Raindrop

Raindrops cling to the railing
a jeweled necklace shimmers
I look away, then look again
fleeting bubbles burst in a blink
glimmers of beauty in this fragile world

Surviving a deluge of falling tears
one raindrop remained
a teardrop shed from gloomy skies
landing on my porch
so I can bear witness to its singular life

Ornamental Grass in Winter

Behold its beauty
strong enough to withstand driving snow and pelting rain
supple enough to sustain the winds of change, the swirling
    storms
delicate enough to rival finely spun lace

For now, you hold space rooted in frozen ground
but soon new shoots will bolt and curl and twirl
around these clumps of dying fronds
behold its beauty

Soul Searching

Candles lit and pillows plumped
Incense wafts about as flutes echo
The cushion gives way as my bones settle
Mind focused, breath steady, spine rigid
Searching for your soul is not an easy quest

Years of seeking and no closer to the goal
Incense cloys the back of my throat
Nostrils twinge as I sniffle and sneeze
Knees creak skyward on rusty hinges
No lotus flower rising from the muck

Just when you think you've grasped
your essence, your soul, your true nature
Poof!
It vanishes like dandelion fluff
Your petty self arises, ego intact

And in charge

The Mad Robin of Fernwood Drive

Her building skills were sloppy
Her flight fast and furious
Furtively she worked all day
Tinsel and twigs tossed askew

The first nest perched behind the lantern
Another above the drain spout
A third wedged between the eaves
By the fourth day twelve more under the rafters

A manic blaze of spring fever?
An avian addiction to serial bigamy?
Was I witnessing a rare nesting disorder?
Should I plan an intervention?

Calling all cardinals, finches and nuthatches
Rescue your sister
Before cluster housing ruins the neighborhood
No room to spread your wings

By the fifth day she limped
Her leg crushed as she charged the glass door
Her glossy breast now dull, her feathers tattered
Her chirping a faint whimper

But by the seventh day she snuggled in her chosen nest
Her dainty head tucked beneath a wing
Her breath steady as she warmed her eggs
Her one true mate keeping watch nearby

Amber Threads

Honey drizzled in a thick amber thread
as my spoon clanked round the teacup rim
A bell tolling
back to the day we brought you home
We looked like biohazard police
in our veiled white suits
You clung to each other, clustered together
So far from home
I was nervous too

Did the smoke make you dizzy?
You tumbled and tripped, spilling as one
How you quivered
when I placed Her among you with
loyal guards to protect the queen
From gentle humming, a buzzing grew
Some waggled, some wiggled
Some washed her feet and spiraled skyward
gleeful to be free

Clever hunters found gold in skunk cabbage
mining pollen buried deep in thorny husks
Days grew warmer
Your pockets burst with pollen as
you flitted from bloom to bloom
I Ommmmed on my approach
You hummmmed in soft reply
I grew primrose, lavender, mint
serving you as you served your queen
My garden divas

Days turned dark, danger lurked
I tried to keep you safe
Fed you sweetwater, kept you warm
There was no clue on the day of the coup
A few rebels grew into an angry swarm
Dense, menacing
No gentle humming, more a drumroll when
one queen surrendered to another

Trees Begin to Weep

When tin pails glint in February sun
Trees begin to weep

Before the pussy willow buds
Before the peepers chirp
A pulse beats, pressure builds
Temperatures rise and maple sap flows

Under the canopy of spring's promise
Tendrils from deepest roots
Lie coiled in darkness
Drawing strength to soar

Earth and sky play tug of war
The balance shifts
A thaw begins
A drip, a trickle, a rush

What slumbered now awakens
Roots pull, sunlight beckons
Magnetic forces strain
Earth exhales a vaporous release

Fire and flame ignite
The balance shifts once more
Golden amber thickens
To a sticky sweet delight

Finding Marsh Marigolds

Garlicky ramps and fiddlehead ferns
cluster in tight swirls, a forager's delight when
new life pokes through rot and
my quest for marsh marigolds begins

Yet another ode to Spring?
isn't that what rebirth is all about?
what love promises
each time like the first time

No primrose path or tiptoeing through tulips
I balance on a shaky boardwalk
oozing life beckons on either side
skunk cabbage unfurls with veins pulsing green

Tree roots heave planks off kilter
Mayday barks and strains her leash
I wobble and totter on this quest that
danger makes more enticing

A chorus of peepers echoes
Mayday pulls, or is it life
tugging me along this twisted path?
stretching to its end I know not where or when

At last, amidst the swamp
clumps of yellow sparkle
each leaf translucent in late day sun
far from pristine lawns and pruned hedges
my elusive treasures hide…marsh marigolds

Cello Sweet

Young cellists clad in black
eyes glistening, confidence gleaming
glossy cellos shining in red, brown, ochre
hold memories of maple and spruce
seeping through grainy pores

Fingers dancing on slender necks
bows gliding over sylvan curves
strings vibrating with celestial sounds
cellist and cello hewn as one
heaven to my ears

A chord touched my heart
a note stopped my breath
a tear trickled down his cheek
for loss, for love, for long ago laments

Solos bubbled through the air
flashing like shooting stars
while de Falla's Spanish Suite swelled

We left enchanted, holding hands
lingering notes wafted through tender leaves
embracing lilacs into the Spring night

Trumpets Call

A trumpet blares atop St. Mary's Basilica
carrying echoes of medieval Krakow when
Tatars pounded at Florian's Gate
until an arrow cut short his alarm
Every hour of every day
The bugler plays but no one hears

Church bells ring, my head spins
Hoofbeats clomp on time worn cobblestones
Sausages sizzle from open braziers
Pushcarts peddle just baked pretzels
Everything and nothing has changed

Eight hundred years since that bugler tumbled
marking Poland's blood soaked roots
stemming from the crossroads of Europe
Mongols, Swedes, Germans, Austrians
and always Russians pushing from the East

Despite drones, clones and cellphones
gigabytes, electrolytes and satellites
strongmen still conquer for power and greed
Fear still spreads on winds of lies
Ears still fall deaf to the trumpet's call

Indigo Wings

Day after day I sit by the window and stare
awaiting your return with its message of hope
where have you been and where did you go?
can you find your way back?

Your home is swept clean of squatter remains
the wren's crude nest
the mouse droppings and spider webs
there's suet cake and meal worms, come

With hope beneath your wings
come pluck my seeds of woe
buried deep and scatter them far
where they cannot grow

You swoop and dart and hover
first a flash, then a flutter
teasing like no other, you vanish
indigo wings dip in a true blue sky

A blush of peach, no orange or is it rose?
no crayon box can match your hue
your spark of joy reignites my soul and
my heart flutters on this bluebird day

Shedding DNA

Two million years ago a mastodon foraged Greenland
shedding DNA in a forest trapped beneath frozen mud
what was, what is, will always be
from mammoth to mouse to microscopic

Matter does not dissolve
what matters does not disappear
the tears we wept, the shrieks of joy
the cries of terror, the kisses blown
the baby's cry, the mother's sigh

Our DNA spirals through the stratosphere
you and I and billions of souls shedding DNA
mounting layer upon layer, never ending
perhaps the ozone hole is an escape hatch
to vent earth's fervent steam

Or perhaps in two million years scientists
will marvel at the detritus of our tears
the echoes of our fears

Note: December 7, 2022 National Geographic: The oldest DNA ever analyzed shows that mastodons and reindeer once wandered a nearly unrecognizable Greenland....2 million years ago it was a forested ecosystem unlike any now found on Earth...

Pan's Legacy

Tread softly and listen for Pan's woodland peepers
stirring treetops to dance in the wind
luring honeybees from winter's slumber
Pan pokes his cloven hoof through oozing muck
a gnarly toenail rising from the forest floor

Sweetness tinged with fertile rot
birthing new life is smelly business
most snub their nose and step around
chopping at his woody root
like Spring he returns again

Deep inside his purple husk
a jealous Pan guards his treasure
eager bees break their fast to fill their sacks
with pollen stolen from within
a golden offering for their queen

Pan's legacy…skunk cabbage

Notre Dame

The gargoyles and chimeras snarl from above
The rooster holds sway upon its spire
silent reminder of St. Peter's betrayal
The portal looms wide as Our Lady opens her arms

Eight hundred years of tears
Eight hundred years of prayers
captured beneath vaulted beams
even a blazing fire couldn't destroy

Our Lady survived it all
Crusaders bearing holy relics
Rebels severing heads of saints and kings
An emperor crowning himself
She, immortal witness from medieval times

Restored to her ancient glory
Our steadfast Lady now trampled
Each day thousands shuffle in a steady stream
A crushing wave no pause to awe in wonder
Stained glass blurred by selfie sticks

A priest sits praying
Alone behind a confessional wall
An empty bench waits
but no one comes to bare their soul
as thousands hustle by

I approach the Crown of Thorns
My footsteps waiver
Aren't holy relics superstitious artifacts?
A hush descends
A holy presence engulfs me

I light a candle for my son
I shed my tears where thousands wept
The buzz becomes a hymn
wrapping me in Her embrace

Recipe for Humanity

Animal, vegetable, mineral
Nature's finest ingredients
Blend to make this human stew
Not sure we have the recipe quite right

Step 1: One part animal

As predators we devour the earth
Conquer foes to suit our need, feed our greed
Beat down the weak, stir up the rest
Yet we suckle our young, protect our nest
Taste love and hate with equal zest

Step 2: Blend with one part vegetable

As plants our cells divide and multiply
Our tender sprouts reach for sun
Our branches spread and wander
With storms some bend, some break
Some grow stronger, we grow to survive

Step 3: Season well

Hearts turn to stone
Cast from sorrow within
Or weighted by chains long ago
We glisten with diamonds in our eyes
We smolder with coal fueling our gut

Step 4: Simmer for a lifetime

Animal, vegetable, mineral
A truly human dish
The taste is off
The smell is foul
Did free will spoil the stew?

Eclipsed

A ring of fire cut a swath across the West
as a scimitar slashed the world in two
eclipsing hope for lasting peace
a schism reaching back through time
since Moses parted the Red Sea

Generations promised to mend the rift
as zealots wreaked havoc with holy wars
revenge begets revenge and the weak suffer
neither global networks nor artificial intelligence
has changed human nature

Ancient prophecies proclaimed
eclipse brought disaster
warning the end was near
when an angry sun rejected heaven
lured by the underworld to lay siege

No food, no water, no shelter
homeless flee on beast and foot
banging pots to scare the demons
as rockets flare and we all fall
into a burning ring of fire

Whalebone Creek

Whalebone Creek cuts a maze through marshland
swathed in gold and blue
wild rice sways, tossing feathery heads
tall reeds nod as if pointing the way
while purple asters reflect in still waters

A chorus of red-winged blackbirds
chirp and feast on sun-dried kernels
red epaulets flash in the sun
clustered two or three to a stalk
hundreds, no thousands come to roost

We dip our paddles without a sound
the lone wood duck stirs
blinded by the sun
I plow into a stand of rice stalks
shadows sway above
rice showers my hair, my shoulders
nature's blessing on this wedding of earth and sky

I savor this moment in autumn light
knowing the days grow short
time stands still for no one
The river can't stop flowing
The world can't stop spinning

But a meander down Whalebone Creek
takes me to a place forgotten by time

Holding

Monarch's Return

You are the One
Slanting sun in the southern sky
draws you closer to its flame
Prisms reflect on tattered wings

The polarity of your soul tugs
The call of the North, the pull of the South
Earth's magnetic lure beckons
over oceans, forests, deserts, plains

One morning ancestral whispers
stir your Aztec roots
murmuring return, return
on the Day of the Dead

Marked for generations
You are the One
You do not question, tarry or delay
You do not ask, will I know the way
to make this date with destiny?

With milkweed poison
to fight the hawk's pursuit,
wings take flight along the shore
Gentle feelers guide the route

Soaring the currents
you spiral up and flutter down
alighting on summer's last blooms
sipping nectar to fuel the way

No border guards can hunt you down
No passport stamps your right of passage
No taunts of alien, you don't belong
No. You are the One

Awaken!

While she slept dreaming
of somewhere over the rainbow
fairies danced around her

They sprinkled dewdrops on her lashes
caressed her lips with warm breezes
but still she slumbered

They laid a pot of gold at her feet
just beyond the rainbow's reach

She slept through the cock's crow
the mourning dove's whoo, who, whoo, who

She slept as the clover turned to the sun
dappled light cast shadows on her nose

The fairies grew bored and drifted away
Their words lingered on treetops,

Awaken! Awaken!

Wooden Spoon

I soften under your warm touch
Grandmother held me, great grandmother too
My roots trace to an old walnut tree
I don't know which one
It was long ago and my memory fades

But when you stir me I know love
Diviner of succulence
Magic wand of nurture
My charred edges now worn smooth
See the crack that never healed

Memories breed deep in my pores
Yeasty breads, cinnamon rolls, simmering stews
Hold me to the light
You might catch a glimpse of
Calico aprons, church socials, Sunday suppers

Stirring, folding, scraping, ladling
Serving generations
Love in a spoonful

Skiing in Yellowstone

Sweat trickled down my spine
Our breath steamed beneath gaiters
I scooped a handful of fresh snow
Icy crystals dissolved on my tongue
Evoking memories of snow cones on a sticky chin

Diamonds shimmered in the valley
Blinding prisms glowed ice blue
So cold, breath shattered in my chest
Our cheeks ruddy red, our noses runny
A distant rumble broke the frozen solitude

We lengthened our strides and rode the glide
Freed by the rhythm of thighs flexing
Like the space between two breaths
An eagle soaring between wing beats

I blinked and blinked again, fog clouded my vision
A massive hulk appeared then disappeared
Shrouded in mist at the bend of the river
Steam billowed from its nostrils and ice clumped its matted hide
With head bowed low, weighed by its hump or its history I'll
    never know

We froze out of wonder
We froze out of fright
We could have been the last creatures on earth
Oblivious, the beast drank its fill then lumbered on
Vanishing into the mist and windswept snow

Onward we skied overcome with awe
To speak would be sacrilege
Beyond the next crest steam rose
Hot breath from earth's core bubbled
I beckoned him to follow and off we dashed

Layer by layer skis and clothes flew helter skelter
We slipped into the swirling hot spring
Transcending space and time
Held buoyant by this moment
This day of unmatched bliss

Wrestling Beauty

You said I painted with flowers
My garden a palate of violets and lilies
Plump tomatoes and ruby berries ripe for the picking
A canvas brushed with beauty

But beauty often follows destruction
Blood root sprouts where the tulip tree fell
Wisteria drapes the dead cedar
Honeysuckle cloaks the broken fence

Wrestling beauty from rocky soil takes work
And more than a shovel of hope
You denied hope, called it 'the panacea of the masses'
But it was clear you had it in spades

Sometimes hope drained like dirty bath water
Leaving stains of grit and scum
I whispered to the whoosh of your oxygen machine
I will create beauty with every step
I will create beauty with every step

With pitchfork in hand and hip waders sinking deep
I saved the pond from a mass of emerald green
Spreading watercress all I could control
Snarled roots piled high while crawfish and frogs
Wriggled to safety in water that ran clear

Then I sat in the grass hunting four-leaf clovers
Listening for the evening song of peepers
And your plaintive cry

Crossing the Line

I cannot not cross the line to save you
I sit, I stare
twirling my wedding ring round and round
until its grip loosens as I spin out of control

Hours pass and I wait alone
Slivers of light through swinging doors reveal no clue
A vending machine and stale coffee sustain me
A ticking clock my only companion

I stare at the crack in the floor
A schism wider than the Grand Canyon
Step on a crack, break your mother's back
The children's rhyme echoes through my brain

Doctors in white coats parade without a glance
Voices hushed and footsteps rushed
Surgical steel and sterile tubes lock you away
My treasure in a vault and I have no key

Together at last in the shadow of your coma
Tubes run in, tubes run out
Click, whoosh, shhh; click, whoosh, shhh
The ventilator drums its staccato beat
My breath syncopated with yours

Click, whoosh, shhh; click, whoosh, shhh
Dripping bags deliver elixirs of life
Can you squeeze my finger?
Just one sign to tell me you're here
as you float beneath the surface ever so near

A shaft of light, the shadow lifts
An eyelash flickers, a tear trickles
You've come back to me across that line
You, the survivor of at least nine lives

Golden Chalice

Sparks flew when the universe popped its cork
An explosive event no ears could yet hear
Thunder roared and cosmic bubbles overflowed
bursting into planets born of darkest matter
colliding and fizzing as embers cooled

Blinded by the light they danced
spinning around the golden orb
Some burned in the cauldron's fiery blaze
Some froze and wandered far from its glow
Only one shimmered in shades of green and blue

Woven in a web of push and pull
each planet found its place
orbiting through time and space
Without the light to hold our gaze
we'd float in darkness all our days

For Jarek: The Tapestry

The son lost the father
and the fabric tore
The father lost the son
and the gaping hole widened

Across time and space
frayed ends dangled
straining to mend the break

A stitch dropped here
a snag caught there
no end to the unraveling

Until the warp of the eternal
and the weft of the earthly
wove together making the tapestry complete

Heart Flutters

Tucked beneath your wing
My fluttering heart steadies
Nestled against your chest and wrapped in down
You keep the night demons at bay
We feather our nest, pecking here, cooing there
With morning's light I take flight
Freed from tethers of fear and loss
To soar on clouds of joy and gusts of laughter

Fault Lines

Sorrow etched your rugged face
Just as fault lines split mountains
The seismic shifts of a stormy life

I trace those crevices blazed long ago
Clue by clue I decipher their hieroglyphics
The joys, the sorrows, the loves lost and found

Tenderly I soothe the wounds of years gone by
Together we travel those well-worn paths
As trailblazers of the heart we chart a new course

You've played many roles, worn many masks
But now you stand unveiled before me
Your past and future forged into now

Hands

A sculptor's hands breed life from stone
A conductor's wand sends music soaring
A fortune teller sees the future in my palm
I see reflections of the past
These purple veins map trails of grit and steel

Gnarled knuckles shine like polished stones
A treasure map of secrets held and prayers begged
If hands could talk they'd tell
stories mouths could never speak

I clasped her toddler hand in mine
dimpled, plump and rose petal soft
She clasped my finger, all her fist could hold
Not yet clenched in fear or wrung with worry

I held his hand, squeezing gently
His pulse the silent world between us
until his life passed into mine
his hand grown cold and still

Listen closely to the stories hands tell
to the secrets held in lives lived well

Yours

Your mouth crushes mine
Like grapes pressed to wine

Your tongue fills my mouth,
Coaxing every crevice, every crease

The bony ridge above my teeth,
    Yours

The tender chord under my tongue,
    Yours

The roof of my palate, skylight to nirvana,
    Yours

The inside of my cheek, slippery and
hidden like the recesses of that special place of desire,
    Yours

I am Yours

The Sculptor

You sculpt my body with hands
speaking a language all their own
    desire
    tenderness
    longing
    seeking
    hunger
And, yes, even

possession

You unlock my secret code
plucking the jewel from my heart
With sleight of hand
my skin turns silky

My tender heart finally exposed
Inside out and upside down

I find there is nothing to hide

Final Bow

Alone on a familiar stage
He bowed to an empty theater
Seventy years since his first applause
New seats, new lights, fresh paint
Can't restore creaky bones and weakened voice
Listen closer
Floorboards seep forgotten lines
Laughter floats from beams above
Sighs whisper after the curtain falls
A piece of him still lingers in the wings
Theater became his life
Tragedy, comedy, romance and farce
All played their roles
But theater saved him and made him whole
Once frightened, excited, humbled and full of hope
Where dreams of success faded to nostalgia
And the passage of time came full circle

Losing

Holding the Light

I have an urge to chase the sun
as it creeps across the autumn sky
to rescue sun-drenched days from darkness
to hold its light as it burns through time

Tugged by a weight too much to bear
sinking as the end draws near
it melts into the horizon
reflecting glory in the crimson sky

Imagine ancient fire carriers
running from hearth to hearth
tending glowing embers
a burning fire their sacred offering

May I too become a lightbearer
tending my embers of love
holding the light until it melts
onto your heart's horizon

Captured in the Cloud

Since time began our thoughts were free to roam
From shepherd's field to actor's stage
Carried by words that swirled and churned
Soft whispers and battle cries
A lover's gasp and father's rage
Gaia listened to it all
She inhaled our woe, exhaled new life
Now, She has had enough

Our thoughts now captured in the Cloud
Lassoed and corralled in desert silos
Temperature controlled holding pens
Where rain and tears can never fall
Nor joy and laughter ever ring
We click and tap from silent screens
Seeking answers to connect
While earbuds block our senses
No wonder Gaia stopped listening

Mirror, Mirror on the Wall

From the inside looking out
my reflection seems the same
An image etched in my mind's eye long ago

Dad's brown eyes dancing with light
My dazzling smile after the braces
A girl cartwheeling through life
sending hearts aflutter

My view of the world is still the same
A tree is meant for climbing
Puddles for jumping
Sunsets for chasing
Stars for wishing

The mirror doesn't lie
From the outside looking in, I wonder who she is
A passing glance, is that mother staring back?
A stranger perhaps, surely not me

Good thing the heart sees no mirrors
It grows with the pulse of love
It melts with the sorrow of tears
and steadies with your hand in mine

Gardeners Lament

Mice nibbled corn plump with summer rain
naked cobs etched with teeth marks
glossy eggplants lay gutted
purple shells blackening in the sun
no aubergine in garlic sauce tonight

Peapods lay splayed open
jade jewels plucked one by one
shredded husks, mocking proof of clever thieves
lacy leaves the holed remains of pole beans
zucchini withered on the vine

A chipmunk froze mid chew
ears perked to babies cries of distress
she scampered beneath nasturtiums
saved to relish another day

Who am I to deny this family their feast?
Aren't we all surviving the best we can?

Uprooted

Their shiny new mailbox should have warned me

No wild strawberries along the path
No creeping thyme between the stones
Where's the brass figa doorknocker?
Good luck symbol to ward off evil

Crooked stones replaced with concrete
New life had clearly taken root
They're expecting their first baby,
It's only fitting they leave their mark

My gardens once rambled in wild abandon
Spilling over stone walls and arbors
Gone are the climbing roses and herb gardens
Giving way to pristine shrubs and a manicured lawn

The copper beech still stands her ground
The weeping willow holds sway over the pond
Marsh marigolds nestle by the stream
Ramps hide safely in the woods

It's not mine any longer…I am uprooted

Transplanted where I now grow
With lady's mantle and columbine
On a rocky ledge by the forest's edge
In a place I love, my new home

Dark Eyed Junco

a dark-eyed junco lies stunned
by the light of a threshold it cannot cross
a beauty unmarred by death
poised this frozen morning on wings
that lift no more

I once watched a pair of tufted titmice
one lying limp on its side
the other, not willing to go on alone,
nudged and prodded, flapped and fluttered
to stir its mate

a hopeless cause I feared
as the strong one stayed and persevered
at last it stood on shaky legs
together again they flew to safety
sheltered from the hawk's watchful eye

my tea brews and thoughts wander
I plead my prayer of flight
I glance again
only a thawing patch of ice remains where
she vanished into the early dawn

Racing Time

Spring races headstrong into summer
a teenager freewheeling downhill
feet on handlebars pedals spinning
cottonwood fluff carries peals of laughter

Can't I linger nose nuzzled in lilacs a moment more?
It's true time waits for no one
Magnolia blossoms turn brown and slimy
Peonies bow their sodden heads to pelting rain

Every spring stirs memories of some past avian life
Furtively I scurry, planting and primping my nest
Is this race against time Newton's other law of gravity?
Though Einstein would say it's all relative

The oak doesn't count its rings
But time carries all we've ever been
From mountain to boulder to stone to pebble
Rolling, tumbling until ashes return to dust

Ashes, ashes we all fall down

The Gift

A young mother and two boys stand in the woods
the forest floor carpeted in autumn leaves
shafts of light stream around them
anointing their crowns in a golden glow

The photo is hazy, softened and blurred by time
heads bowed in silent reverie
hands cupped in open prayer
to receive an offering, nature's sacrament
perhaps a toad, an acorn, a fallen leaf?

Memories of that day fade with passing years
I see now the gift was not a toad, an acorn or fallen leaf
but a mother's gentle touch
planting seeds of wonder in young boys hearts

Rise and Fall

The sun neither rises nor sets
It is the earth that turns towards and away

Surely, though, the moon must rise
Sometimes full, often in shadow
Pulling tides with her gravity

Birdsong rises and hawks descend
Angers rise and people march
Fists rise and nations crumble

Waves crest then crash
Fog rises then fades
As vaporous as each breath dissolving

I rise and fall within each breath
Joy or sorrow within each gasp
Holding them in equal measure

The paradox of a balanced life

Yet once we take our final fall
To rise again defies the law
The eternal question remains

Did He rise?
How can it be?
Will we?

Madness Coiled

Did madness lurk all this time?
Coiled, waiting to strike
Its viperous tongue tasting despair
sensing your breaking point

A sleeping menace, watching for decades
before its crushing blow sent
poison spewing from your words
wreaking havoc in a manic rage

Did you live in silent fear?
Fighting inner demons, overcoming obstacles
The harder you worked, the more patient it grew
knowing its moment would come

Did I believe what I wanted to believe?
I thought the diagnosis wrong
How lost you must have felt
I long to right all the wrong turns

You are not defined by that long ago past
You have slain the beast that lurked
Now throw open your windows
And let your light shine out

Still

Be still, hear rain pelt the pane
Still enough to hear branches wrestle the wind
Skies so full of woe they overflow with
weeping at so much strife below
What are my tears in comparison?

Still they are my tears

Rain needles my brain with questions
Why so much grief?
Why so much pain?
Why so much sorrow?
I know mine pales to the world's

Still it is my grief, my pain, my sorrow

Be still after the storm and listen
Woodpeckers drill and crickets chirp
Teapots whistle and clocks tick
Bees buzz and highways hum

Still

Prickers

Like a hyena tearing guts from fresh kill
I yank snarled prickers by the root
attacking each cane with vengeance
Sweat soaks my shirt, my mouth is dry

Thorns poke through thick gloves
I flinch, yet welcome the pain
Pinpricks of blood seep through my sleeve
leaving constellations of sorrow and woe

You are tangled in a web of despair
unable to set yourself free
strangled by a disease no pruning can sever
I am helpless to fix your life

I toil on, beating this target for my rage
but this pain cannot be purged
My mindless task becomes obsessive
The stack of prickers pile high above my head

Yellowjackets swarm, I cry
Stabbing pain burns my ankles, thighs
Hands swell
The blade in my heart cuts deeper
I take cover fleeing to safe haven

Where oh where is yours?

When Did You Become You?

Was it when you were a five day old embryo first learning to swim?
Or when you reached the primitive streak transforming from potential to life?
Was it when you scratched with nails grown too long in the womb?
Or your tottering first steps, eager for a vertical perspective?

When did you first know this world was too harsh for you?
Was it when your tattered blankie dissolved leaving you in tears?
Or your first heartbreak when your father left?
Was it when you ran away but couldn't escape yourself?

When did you become you?
I know it was when you became a dad
I saw your love rise like a swelling tide
And you learned to swim again

Golden Boy

The first beach day when pores open to the sun's kiss
when the promise of languid summer days yawns wide
timeless as the forever boys racing to the jetty's end
scampering over craggy rocks, muck oozing between toes
backs bent low plucking crabs from tidal pools
my vision was hazy, dazed in the noonday sun
it had to be you in all your boyhood glory
honey curls whipped in unruly waves to rival the sea
shoulders mere buds of broad muscles soon to grow
body yet to catch up with coltish legs
back dusted with brown sugar sand
cast in bronze and frozen in time
you balanced on rocks, eyes searching the horizon
you turned, waved to pals on shore and vanished from view
…a passing cloud broke the spell…

two weeks later you vanished for good
had you come to say goodbye, my golden boy of summer?

Darkness Shed

Long ago a parasite of darkness burrowed deep within
Like a cicada it hid cocooned in its thick shell
Brooding, conspiring, worming its way and waiting
Waiting to reemerge at your weakest moment

Once it spread its wings of venom
A veil clouded your vision
Its vaporous fog poisoned your brain
Infected the air you breathed
Coursed through your veins and smothered love

Feeding off your goodness, the darkness deepened
Your inner light dimmed
Your eyes deadened in empty sockets
Your voice flattened as you choked on words
Strangled from within

The darkness was a jealous lover
Claiming you for its own
Blocking out all who loved you
Severing even the love for your children

The darkness won
I know you had no choice

Who can live without the light?
Without the nourishment of forgiveness?
Without tears to wash away our sorrow?
Without love to embrace our hearts?
To hold and be held

You became a hollow cocoon, a wooden puppet
If only I were a master carpenter with a magic wand as my chisel
If only I were a gallant knight victorious in slaying the dragon
If only I could click my ruby slippers to bring you home

But I am only a mother
Longing to hold you one last time
To birth your spirit into the light
Where darkness is forever banished

Erin's Sign

Give me a sign to take away my doubt
Help me believe this isn't the end
For nothing ends without a new beginning

A tree falls and mushrooms grow, violets bloom
New life spreads across the forest floor
as surely as its branches once reached the sky

A raindrop doesn't disappear when thrust from its cloud to
merge with the river, becoming one with the ocean
It is still there, embraced in all that is

But your cold blue touch gave me no sign
Heavy with the weight of the undeniable,
I stumbled home in a fog of disbelief

The front door loomed, gateway to my new unknown
And there before me, impossible to miss,
something blue clung to the door — a flower? a burst balloon?

Before me wings spread, iridescent and transparent
Wet from birth, a blue cicada emerged from its shell
discarding what it no longer needed

It took flight, soaring on currents where I cannot go
Its haunting song trailed from treetops
a sacred gift from the Muses

I need no further sign than your parting gift of eternity

Author's note: In ancient times from Asia to Greece, cicadas symbolized rebirth and immortality. A blue cicada the rarest of all.

Coalescence

From East and West, North and South
your gravitational pull hugged our family tight
bound not by blood, but by love
We laughed and cried and held you to the light

Each a single star shining in solitary worlds
until you drew us to your orbit coalescing into
a new constellation for only one day
We followed you, our North Star

Boyhood buddies on skateboards forever soaring
A brother reunited, lost no more to time and distance
A father's wounds healed and soothed
Daughters stoic in awe and quiet grief

We beckoned ancestors to guide your way
Told stories to bring you close
Baby, boy, man and father swirled as one
Kaleidoscope images of a soul made whole

Fragmented no more, all barriers erased
By dawn the constellation vaporized
Each star resumed its former orbit
But contrails of your flight linger still

The Box

The box arrived yesterday or maybe the day before
I shoved it in a corner and dared not cross its path
until its contents cried out, longing to be heard

I cradle your silver baby cup
Your name blackened with tarnish
I polish until my hands cramp but
no matter how hard I rub
I can't wipe away my tears
I rub my thumb along the dented bottom
touch the grooves gently
like tickling baby toes

How you banged that cup!
We could barely cover rent and oh how
we laughed — our boy born with a silver spoon
What dreamers we were!
How you banged that cup!

Now your name is engraved on another stone
I can't grasp how this happened
I dig deeper and cry the howl of the wounded
Your teddy bear, one-eyed and matted
His paws reaching to be hugged
I hold him to my nose
hoping your boyhood smell lingers
You slept with that bear longer than you'd admit
but I knew

How can your life fit in a box?
Camp badges and soccer ribbons
Photos and journals, drawings and cartoons
The tumbling angels you played with at Christmas
The stocking I made when you were six

But your life is not in that box
It is all around me and in me

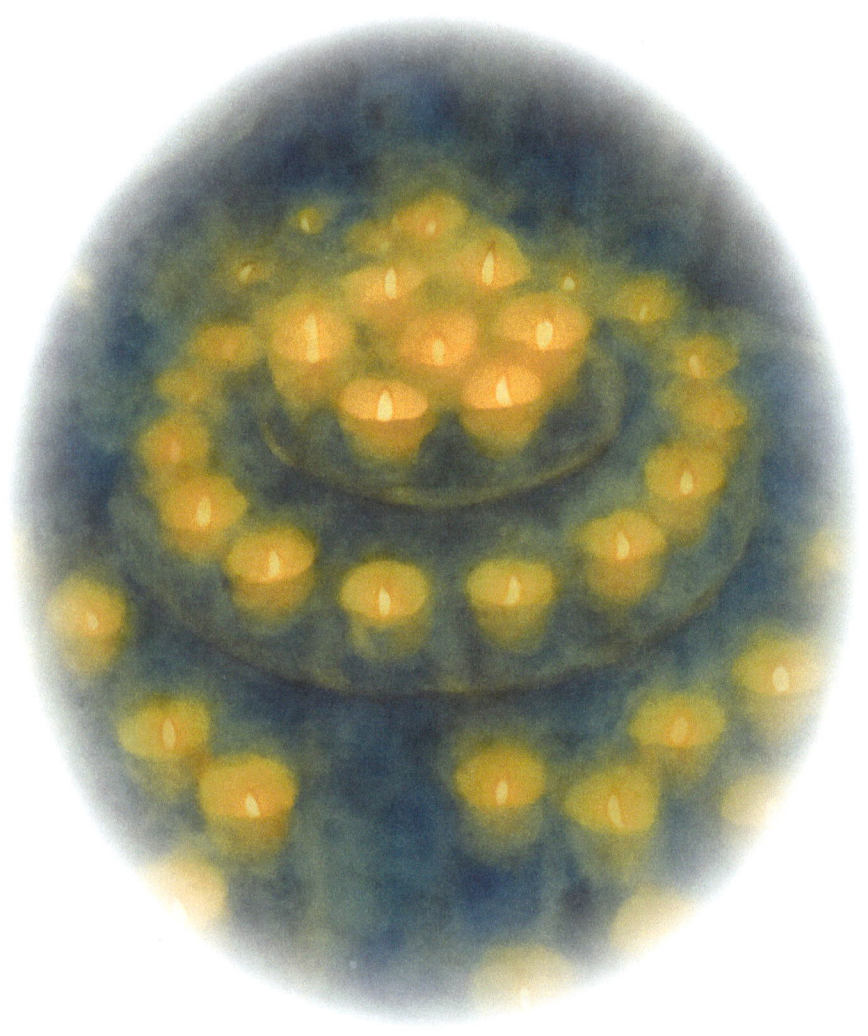

What If?

Dust motes float on a shaft of light and I wonder
What if?

What if our souls are made of particle dust
drifting through the cosmos seeking respite
drawn by magnetic forces coded deeper than DNA?

Soul clusters coalescing into a star
a family helix that reaches back through time
to embrace you in its fold and expand its glow

What if your great great grandfather,
who rode with Pancho Villa to free the downtrodden,
takes you sky riding to lasso comets?

What if your great great grandmother,
who tamed the prairie with a rolling pin and shovel
sings you lullabies around a solar flare?

What if all who you've lost and
all those you never knew
are waiting with a place made just for you?

Find your way to that soul-studded star and wait for me
we'll shine for a million years and
our light will shine for a million more

INDEX OF POEMS

Amber Threads	10	Ornamental Grass	
Awaken!	34	in Winter	7
Captured in the Cloud	56	Pan's Legacy	21
Cello Sweet	16	Prickers	68
Coalescence	75	Racing Time	61
Crossing the Line	40	Recipe for Humanity	24
Dark Eyed Junco	60	Rise and Fall	64
Darkness Shed	72	Shedding DNA	20
Eclipsed	27	Skiing in Yellowstone	37
Erin's Sign	74	Soul Searching	8
Fault Lines	45	Still	67
Final Bow	51	The Box	76
Finding Marsh Marigolds	15	The Gift	63
For Jarek: The Tapestry	43	The Mad Robin of	
Gardeners Lament	58	Fernwood Drive	9
Golden Boy	71	The Sculptor	49
Golden Chalice	42	Trees Begin to Weep	13
Hands	46	Trumpets Call	17
Heart Flutters	44	Uprooted	59
Holding the Light	55	Watch Hill on Indian Lake	5
Indigo Wings	19	Whalebone Creek	29
Madness Coiled	65	What If?	79
Mirror, Mirror on the Wall	57	When Did You Become	
Monarch's Return	33	You?	69
Moon Swallows	6	Wooden Spoon	35
Notre Dame	22	Wrestling Beauty	39
One Raindrop	7	Yours	47

ACKNOWLEDGMENTS

Without the encouragement of the Guilford Poets Guild, I would never have given voice to the thoughts and emotions that swirl in my brain. I especially thank Gordy Whiteman, Guilford's Poet Laureate for many years, whose wisdom and wit shaped the Guild. Nan Meneely's sharp editing skills gave structure to my ramblings. Marie Hulme has encouraged my writing since we became roommates in Fairfield University's MFA program. I thank Jen Payne and Colin Sterling whose technical wizardry helped craft the publication of *Holding The Light*. I thank Amy Barry and our Thursday Writing Group (Kate, Dawn, Joanna, Kristi, Dody and Gayle) for providing the caring support and honest critique every writer needs. My loving partner, Jarek, eagerly read every poem, often before his first cup of coffee. 'Less is more' became his mantra — a lesson I'm afraid I'm still learning.

And lastly, to my late son Andy. The poems that bubbled forth helped pull me from the depths of sorrow.

Sharon Austin Bloom

Sharon went from predicting corn crop production in Illinois to inspecting chicken farms in Alabama to hedging commodity futures on the Chicago Board of Trade. From there she launched a career as a marketing executive in the food industry, while raising her two boys. A move to Connecticut brought a life changing shift to teach yoga and keep bees. And after years of writing ad copy, sales presentations and marketing plans, she finally pursued her dream to become a writer earning an MFA in Creative Writing. She is honored to be copresident of the Guilford Poets Guild and on the Board of Dudley Farm Museum. She lives in Guilford, Connecticut, with her partner, Jarek, and her dog, Mayday.

www.ingramcontent.com/pod-product-compliance
Lightning Source LLC
Chambersburg PA
CBHW042341150426
43196CB00001B/11